Dogs With Jobs

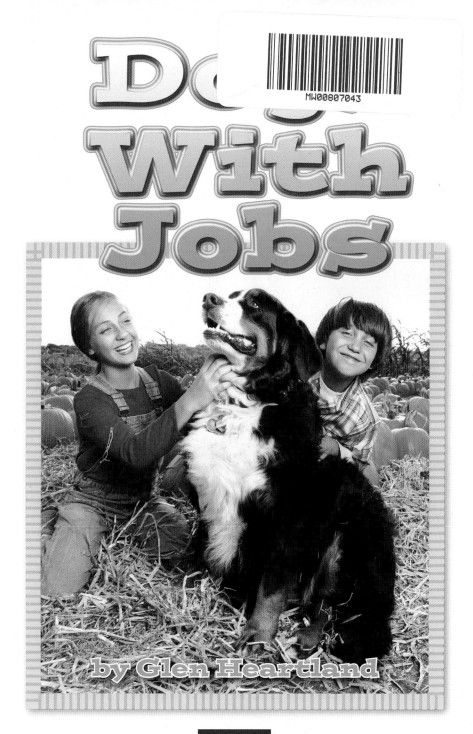

by Glen Heartland

PEARSON

Glenview, Illinois • Boston, Massachusetts • Chandler, Arizona
Upper Saddle River, New Jersey

Man's best friend

"A dog is man's best friend." That's what some people say.

Dogs may also be people's best helpers. Some dogs are trained to help people. These dogs have jobs.

What does the dog smell?

Dogs have a great sense of smell. They smell much better than people can.

Footprints leave light smells behind. Dogs can smell footprints—even old ones.

Dogs smell things on the ground. They smell things in the air. They smell things miles away. They smell things people cannot smell.

A dog smells the ground.

People train dogs to find lost people. Saint Bernards work high in the mountains. They smell people lost in the snow. They help to save lives.

Saint Bernard dog

Dogs make good guards. Farmers train dogs to guard their animals. The dogs keep the animals safe.

Dogs guard farm animals.

Dogs also herd animals. They move sheep or cows from one place to another. A farmer can be away. The dog can still herd.

Herding sheep

This dog works in the city. He keeps geese out of parks. Geese can hurt the grass. The dog herds the geese. It keeps geese away.

Herding geese

Dogs can help on a farm. Some farm dogs keep animals in. Some farm dogs keep animals out. Some find lost animals. Some watch over children. Dogs are great helpers!

Dogs do many jobs.

Service dogs help people with special needs. People who are blind cannot see. The dogs help them walk across streets. They keep the people safe outdoors.

Service dogs help people who cannot see.

Service dogs also help people who are deaf. People who are deaf cannot hear. A car horn may blow. A person who is deaf will not hear the sound. A service dog will hear it. Right away, the dog tells its owner.

Service dogs help people who cannot hear.

Dogs have important jobs. They do things people cannot do. They help people. They keep people safe. Dogs are also great friends!

Dogs are friends.